I0808282

ARENA EVENTS

X GAMES

KENNY ABDO

Fly!
An Imprint of Abdo Zoom
abdobooks.com

abdobooks.com

Published by Abdo Zoom, a division of ABDO, P.O. Box 398166, Minneapolis, Minnesota 55439.

Printed in the United States of America, North Mankato, Minnesota.
092018
012019

THIS BOOK CONTAINS RECYCLED MATERIALS

Photo Credits: Alamy, AP Images, Icon Sportswire, iStock, Shutterstock
Production Contributors: Kenny Abdo, Jennie Forsberg, Grace Hansen
Design Contributors: Dorothy Toth, Neil Klinepier

Library of Congress Control Number: 2018946211

Publisher's Cataloging-in-Publication Data

Names: Abdo, Kenny, author.
Title: X Games / by Kenny Abdo.
Description: Minneapolis, Minnesota : Abdo Zoom, 2019 | Series: Arena events | Includes online resources and index.
Identifiers: ISBN 9781532125409 (lib. bdg.) | ISBN 9781641856850 (pbk) | ISBN 9781532126420 (ebook) | ISBN 9781532126932 (Read-to-me ebook)
Subjects: LCSH: ESPN X-Games--Juvenile literature. | Extreme Games--Juvenile literature. | Extreme sports--Juvenile literature.
Classification: DDC 796.046--dc23

TABLE OF CONTENTS

X GAMES

Putting the X in extreme, the ESPN X Games have thrilled fans of action sports for more than 20 years!

MONSTER
GAMES
AUSTIN
20 YEARS

With exciting tricks, loud music, and pure **adrenaline**, the X Games takes the world by storm in the summer and winter every year.

PLAZA
GAMES
BOTTLES & CANS
COMPOST
TRASH
COMPOST
TRASH

OPENING ACT

Sporting **competitions** have been a source of entertainment for a long time. One of the first was the Cotswold Games. It was held in England in 1612.

ESPN launched the X Games in 1995. It was originally called the Extreme Games. The festivities were held in Rhode Island. It drew more than 200,000 fans. **Competitions** included skateboarding, BMX biking, and motocross.

DEW

It was originally supposed to be a **biennial competition**. But, people liked the X Games so much, it became a yearly event. The summer X Games are held all around the world every August. Athletes compete for gold, silver, and bronze medals. They can also win cash prizes.

ROCKSTAR
ENERGY DRINK

HJC
RCS
D&D
RCS
TRACTION
STUD BOY
ARCTIC CAT
68

The first Winter X Games were held in California in 1997. It featured snowboarding, skiing, and snowmobiling. Challengers in each sport **faced off** in many **competitions**.

THE MAIN EVENT

Athletes have **debuted** new tricks at the X Games. Tony Hawk landed the legendary 900 on his skateboard in 1999. At 12 years old, Tom Schaar landed the 1080 in 2012. It has been called the "Holy Grail of all skateboard tricks."

THE REAL COST
MONSTER
ENERGY

At just 18 years old, Chloe Kim had already won four gold medals at the Winter X Games. She made history in 2016 at the Park City Grand Prix. Kim landed back-to-back 1080s and earned a perfect 100 point score.

X GAMES
X GAMES
THE REAL COST
GAMES
SHREDHATE

The 2018 X Games in Minneapolis offered the first-ever live stream of the events in immersive **virtual reality** (VR). A total of 48 countries around the world were able to experience the rush as if they were there!

GLOSSARY

adrenaline – a natural stimulant in your body that acts as a boost of energy.

biennial – taking place every other year.

competition – an event where people compete in skill.

debut – a first appearance.

face-off – to be in direct competition with people or groups.

virtual reality – a interactive, computer-generated environment experienced through a helmet with a screen inside.

ONLINE RESOURCES

Booklinks
NONFICTION NETWORK
FREE! ONLINE NONFICTION RESOURCES

To learn more about X Games, please visit abdobooklinks.com. These links are routinely monitored and updated to provide the most current information available.

INDEX